Mirrors on Earth

Andrea C. Dexter LSW

Scripture quotations marked (NLT) are taken from the Holy Bible, New Living Translation, copyright ©1996, 2004, 2007, 2013, 2015 by Tyndale House Foundation. Used by permission of Tyndale House Publishers, Inc., Carol Stream, Illinois 60188. All rights reserved.
Scripture quotations are from the ESV® Bible (The Holy Bible, English Standard Version®), copyright © 2001 by Crossway, a publishing ministry of Good News Publishers. Used by permission. All rights reserved.

Scripture is taken from the New King James Version®. Copyright © 1982 by Thomas Nelson. Used by permission. All rights reserved.

Scripture quotations are taken from the Amplified® Bible (AMP), Copyright © 2015 by The Lockman Foundation Used by permission. www.Lockman.org
Scripture quotations are taken from the New American Standard Bible® (NASB), Copyright © 1960, 1962, 1963, 1968, 1971, 1972, 1973, 1975, 1977, 1995 by The Lockman Foundation
Used by permission. www.Lockman.org

Mirrors on Earth

Edited by Freelanceplus
ISBN 978-0-578-43863-4

Acknowledgments

I want to thank my parents, Al Dexter and Barbara Dexter, for encouraging us to attend service and taking us to church every Sunday as children. Thank you for seeking and serving the Lord before us. Your support and love for us have always been a safety net to all of us.

To my siblings—May we all confidently walk in our gifts and callings.

Thank you to my Aunts and Uncles that work in the ministry, continue to walk upright before us, and leave an inheritance of righteousness.

Thank you to my Pastor; Elder Lester Pittman and First Lady, Jelinda Pittman, for showing us perseverance and determination. I also appreciate the Associate Pastors and my church family for studying the Word, giving revelation of the Scriptures in Sunday School and through weekly sermons.

Thank you to Missionary Ollie Brent, Dean of C.H. Mason Bible College, Lawrence County MS branch. Thank you for making Bible courses available and affordable for individuals who are seeking more knowledge of the Scriptures. Thank you to the instructors; Elder Anthony Smith and Elder Glenn Allen, for breaking down the scriptures in a way that everyone could understand.

Thank you to Jennifer Marion and The Center of Empowerment in helping me navigate the book publishing world, I appreciate your help.

TABLE OF CONTENTS

Preface

Write the Vision, Make it Plain, and Wait for it because it will surely come.

Habakkuk 2:2-3

The Lord gave me the vision of this book around 2010, while my pastor was praying over the congregation. The vision was specific in the details, imagery of the cover and the title. I was totally overwhelmed. In this vision, I saw a book cover with my name and credentials on the front as the author. The illustrations on the front and back were blue skies over a field of wheat, with mirrors faced toward the sky as the sun reflected off the front of the mirrors. On the back of the book, it was the same scene but the mirrors were replaced by people of different nationalities, shape, and sizes. Now, honestly, I wasn't rejoicing over this vision. I actually tried to hide this from everyone, including myself. When the Lord would bring it back to my remembrance, I responded with the excuse that I was too busy. I can remember speaking on one occasion in a program about God's purpose for our lives and the phrase "God gave me a book" was about to come out of my mouth and I hurriedly ended so that nobody could hold me accountable for what I said and I would not have verbally acknowledged the vision. It wasn't until October 24, 2016, during the recess of my personal activities and endeavors did the Lord say to me, "You never wrote down the vision." So, I began to write the vision as the Lord previously revealed. But the more I wrote, the more He revealed to me about this book. As I attended Worship services and Sunday School, the Lord gave me more revelation on how to incorporate the scriptures into the book He had given to me. When I needed resources to birth this book, He placed resources in my path to glean. When I needed information on how to publish this book, He gave it to me. Now, I am no longer overwhelmed nor am I hiding the vision. I am actually honored to be the person through whom God chose to push this vision into the earth. He could have chosen anyone, but He chose the person who almost did not graduate high school (not many people knew that tidbit of information) to complete a book. I present to you the Lord's vision in its completed form. I am confident in saying absolutely nothing is impossible for God.

Introduction

I have been in and around church my entire life. My mother is the Sunday School teacher; she taught Sunday School while she was pregnant with me (I have literally been in church my whole life). I remember my siblings and myself winning the perfect attendance award for being in Sunday School every Sunday. I can also remember getting punished as a child because I said that I hated church. (As a child, I thought we went entirely too much.) I have come from a heritage of Christian teachings, Christian ways of life, and customs. Even though I had these role models in Christianity, I was still unsure of how to simply exist as a Christian. Often, I wondered was I supposed to imitate my Grandma Helen, who was a wife, Church Mother, deaconess, entrepreneur, and a caregiver? Or was I supposed to emulate my Grandma Rachel (Red) who was a wife, Church Mother, prophetess, and a prayer warrior? Both were mighty women of God, both women loved God and His Word, but the question remained, should my life mirror their lives?

Why Mirrors?

Every day at some point, each one of us passes a mirror. In each passing, we examine our appearance which includes our, our outfits, and our make-up. For me: I examine the outfit to see if it fits correctly. I also check the mirror for lipstick on my teeth or to see if my hair is neat and kept. Why do I do this? I do this daily ritual because I want to see how I present myself in the public view. How would you know what you look like if you don't look in the mirror? Mirrors in the simplest form can only reflect the images in front of them. If darkness is in front of the mirror, the mirror can only reflect darkness. If light is in front of the mirror, the mirror will reflect light. When you look in the mirror, do you expect to see your next door neighbor looking back at you? No, you see yourself. When you look at your Spiritual self in the mirror of the Word, do you see the image of Christ?

First Natural, Then Spiritual

… If there is a natural body, there is also a spiritual body (I Cor. 15:44; ESV)

...But it is not spiritual that is first, but the natural and then the spiritual (I Cor. 15;46; ESV)

One of the unwritten characteristics of God is an Architect. Since the creation of the world, God has been a God of order and structure. You can see this principle in the six days of Creation described in the first chapter of Genesis. Later, you see the same principle of order and structure when God gives detailed instructions to Noah on building the Ark. God uses His architectural skill to create Adam and then uses the same blueprint to create the Church (For just as the body is one and yet has many parts, and all the parts, though many, form [only] one body, so it is with Christ. I Cor. 12:12; AMP). God, in His infinite wisdom, to show us order, foundational truth and structure, used Paul to write these words: "First natural then spiritual."

My endeavor in this book will be to examine every area of the body as it relates to how we are to reflect the glory of God in the body of Christ, and how we are to use the physical body to reflect the glory of God in the earth.

Chapter 1

The Head

... But be transformed by the renewing of YOUR mind... (Romans 12:2; NASB)

In the beginning the earth was without form and void... (Gen.1:2). When a child is born, its mind is void of structure and order. The child only knows that its body has basic essential needs that have to be met. The child has no other way to express their needs to be met other than crying. It is the parents or caregiver's job to structure and influence the blank canvas of the child's mind to the tendency of God (Prov. 22:6; KJV).

The average adult brain is usually three pounds in weight; it is the central command for our body.[1] The brain is the largest and most complex part of the nervous system. If you want your left finger to punch a key on the cell phone, your brain must tell it to do so first before it could complete this action. The brain on average has about seventy thousand thoughts per day. If you are like me, it would be safe to say all those thoughts do not reflect God. Have you noticed how your mind wanders when you are bored? Have you noticed how non-productive you are when your mind is on a wandering tangent? I have observed my actions whenever my mind wanders away. I am usually in one spot scrolling through social media; my eyes are fixed on the screen of my cellular phone. This is because the command center is not giving any thoughts that would produce actions to the body. When the mind is idle, the body is usually idle.

How does God think?

For my thoughts are not your thoughts, neither are your ways my ways, declares the Lord (Isa. 55:8).

Ever since the fall of man, humans have an inherently sinful nature. One does not have to be taught sin; we already know how to do it from birth. Our actions and our thoughts vastly differ from God's thoughts and actions. The comparison of the human mindset and perspectives are by default flawed and beneath the mindset of GOD. The Bible gives several examples of the thoughts of God based on His actions.

"For God so loved the world that he gave his only begotten Son, that whosoever believeth in him should not perish, but have everlasting life" (John 3:16; KJV).

Let's be honest, would you have given your only beloved child as a sacrifice to save the lives of others? I would have a hard time fulfilling that request. Another example of God's thinking is shown in the Book of Isaiah. Here is an invitation to the thirsty to come and enjoy the richest of fare, enjoy food without cost, wine that one does not have to pay to drink, and experience an eternal covenant that was promised to our forefathers (Isaiah 55:1-5; NIV).

It is apparent that the foundation of God's thoughts process can be expressed by two words; love and covenant. Only love could continue to give, beckon you to come without resources to give back. Only love could allow God to give His best gift as a sacrifice for our sins. Only the unconditional love of God could keep His covenant to us.

How can we obtain thoughts and a mindset that represents God?

The Bible says, "Be ye transformed by the renewing of your minds" …

(Romans 12:2; KJV). Do you realize that everything begins with a thought

or idea? In the Book of Genesis, man was an exchange of ideas manifested

by words spoken within in the Trinity before he was made to appear on

the earth (Genesis 2:5-8). Absolutely, everything begins as an idea. Our

houses, clothes, automobiles, books, etc., started as an idea before it

evolved into a finished product. Even the action of sinning begins with a

thought or idea. Our old mindset is like Adam and Eve's; we want to fulfill

the lust of the flesh despite God's command to us. If Adam and Eve's

thoughts were fixed upon doing what God's commanded regardless of the

situation they faced, our world would be entirely different. Their decision

not to obey God's command began with a thought of doubt which

produced their action to eat what was commanded for them not to eat in

the Garden of Eden (Gen. 3:4-5). Their disobedience yielded sin in the

earth. In order for our thoughts to reflect God, our minds must be

renewed. Our minds must be established again, or reset to accept, grasp,

and comprehend Godly morals and ordinances. Since we are born with a

sinful nature and mindset, in order to be changed, we have to be born again (John 3:3). Parallel to the uninfluenced mind of a newborn, the canvas of the born again mind has to be painted with God's Word. God's Word has the power to reset the mind, give it the ability to grasp the principles in the Bible, and re-establish the thought patterns of the mind. The Bible is full of life-changing information and spirit-filled Word to produce transformation (Heb. 4:12). The "Bread of Life" is to the spiritual body; as the bread of the table is to the natural body. They are both sources of nourishment that must be ingested daily. The Word of God shows how men and women faced and overcame challenges as they learned of the faithfulness of God.

When the Lord places new information and revelation regarding His Word in your path, you are responsible for internalizing and giving action as a response to accepting this new information. The Lord knows the very intent of your heart. He knows if you sincerely want to understand His Word. The nature of God is to be a provider for His people (Jehovah Jireh); the Lord will make provisions and lead you to obtain a better understanding of His word like a "Good Shepherd" would by leading his sheep to food.

Today, the Word of God is so readily available that there are no excuses not to have access to the Word of God. There are Bible apps on cell phones and tablets, Sunday School lessons videos online, sermons on the Internet, and many churches worldwide are broadcasting their services live weekly. These are all tools you can use to daily obtain new insight and revelation about God's spirit-filled word, and as a result, the mind will be transformed to reflect God's nature in your thinking. You may be like I was at one point: I could read the Bible, but I did not understand what it meant. The Bible says you have not because you ask not (James 4:2). If you want a better understanding of His word, ask God in prayer. The Lord is faithful to forgive sin, supply our needs, and renew our minds.

"Kill the Head—The body is Dead"

When we were children, my dad would give us tips on defending ourselves against bullying or fighting. He would tell us to strike in the head to get the opponent off balance and then continually hit the rest of the body because if you kill the head, the body is dead. This is the same strategy satan uses on the physical body and the body of Christ today. The devil knows it is with the mind that we serve the Lord (Roman 7:25). The devil uses strategies to keep the mind preoccupied with obsessive damaging thoughts. Satan uses blows of depression, anxiety, worry, stress, low self-esteem, a defeated mentality, and poor self image to get us off balance in our view of who God has called us to become and sadly, some of us never fully develop into the person God destined us to become. Although depression, anxiety, stress, worry, low self-esteem, and poor self-image are issues based in the mind, they can be a direct link to diagnosis that occurs in natural the body. Hypertension, heart attacks, chest pains, obsessive behaviors, stomach ulcers, and even suicide can be the by-product of depression, stress, and anxiety. If you watch the news daily, read the newspaper daily or even scroll through social media long enough, one can become bombarded with negative influences, images, and information that can leave you thinking that there is nothing in which we should hope. The devil knows that it is with the mind that we serve the Lord and it is satan's job description to steal, kill, and destroy. So, if we allow satan to steal our peace, destroy our joy, he could kill the body. This is why it is essential to keep your mind on God and God's word: as the scriptures say, He will keep you in perfect peace. *Thou wilt keep him in perfect peace, whose mind is stayed on thee: because he trusteth in thee.* (Isaiah 26:3; KJV).

"Finally, brethren, whatsoever things are true, whatsoever things are honest, whatsoever things are just, whatsoever things are pure, whatsoever things are lovely, whatsoever things are of good report; if there be any virtue, and if there be any praise, think on these things" (Philippians 4:8). The way we are to reflect God's glory in our minds is to have a renewed mindset. We are to let this mind be in us as it is in Christ Jesus.

Chapter 1 Challenge: Commit to memory Philippians 4:8 and when you begin to feel anxious, overwhelmed, or worried: recite aloud and activate the scripture in your mind.

Let us pray,

Lord, you are all-knowing, ever-present, and everlasting. Lord, help us to reflect you in our thoughts, decisions, and actions. Lord, give us an unsettling yearning to want to know you more deeply in our thinking. Lord, give us unction by your Holy Spirit to seek you the more. Lord, I ask that you give us burning ears and heart for your Word, and we will continue to give you all the glory, honor, and praise. In Jesus' name, Amen.

Chapter 2

The Entry Points to the Mind:

Eyes, Ears, Nose & Mouth

"The light of the body is the eye: if therefore thine eye be single; thy whole body shall be full of light.[23] *But if thine eye be evil; thy whole body shall be full of darkness. If therefore the light that is in thee be darkness, how great is that darkness!" (Matthew 6:22-23).*

Our eyes, mouth, nose, and ears are entry points by which we decipher information through our senses. Our eyes were created so that we can see the beautiful colors of the rainbow. Our mouth can speak sweet words to others and taste the sweetness of candy. Our ears can listen to the melodic tones of music, and hear calming words of God in our spirit. And with the nose, we can smell the delightful scent of Gardenias. By these entry points, we take in information, we form perspectives about colors, the taste of different foods, the actual sounds of music, and decide what smells we enjoy. This perspective is processed, stored in our brain, and is used as a reference point for the next time we see, taste, hear, or smell. Our minds goes back to that stored reference point where we can recall every emotion attached to the perspective. Therefore, Christians must protect their gates; we must guard what goes in and out of these points of entry.

The natural use of our eyes is to allow images to be introduced into the brain; which is the method by which we obtain information (in a nutshell). Although the eye is used for vision, the eyes also help with balance and ambulation. For example; have you ever gotten up to use the bathroom at two in the morning and there was no light in the room, and you stumbled over a chair in your room or hit your toe on the edge of the bed? It's the same chair that was there in the daytime hours; nothing changed; it's in the exact same spot before you turned off the lights and fell asleep. Nothing about the chair changed, the variable is your ability to see it clearly. If you were able to see, you would not have knowingly walked into a chair. When the eyes are clear, you have perfect vision. Minor missteps like stumbling over obstacles become obsolete when you have clear vision. In Hosea 4:5, the writer speaks of God's chosen people falling in the daytime and the prophets stumbling by night. Both groups are supposed to have the ability to see what is to come. The prophet

Hosea is speaking about God's chosen people being unable to see, not because they are naturally blind but because they are spiritually blind. They are blind to the Word and the ways of God. The Word says I am the way, the truth, and the life (John 14:6). In Hosea 4:5, Israel decided not to choose the truth or the life, but rather, they chose to commit adultery and follow after other gods. As a result of their ignorance and blindness, they stumbled and fell. Deciding to stay blind to the truth of God, the way of God, and the life of God, will keep you tripping over the same thing, in the same spot. Imagine the person with cataracts, the cloudy film that covers the lens hinders everything they view. Simple task like driving at night becomes difficult, and colors are not as bright because there is something that blocks clear sight. The way we can reflect God in our eyesight is to allow the Light of Truth to brighten our path so that we will not stumble and fall.

When the eye is single

Have you ever focused on something so hard that you could not hear others in the background talking to you? It was as if you are in a zone where your entire body is concentrating and working toward the one thing your eyes are focused on. This is what "if thine eye be single" looks like; this level of concentration is so intense that it causes all of your being to be channeled to accomplish one common goal. If one fully focuses on God with a concentration that is channelled only toward our love for Him, the environment around us dissipates.

What we watch on television has an impact on our "singleness of eye;" we have to guard the eye gate. Watching derogatory television shows and pornographic images will stunt the growth of the Christian by introducing perversion through the eye gate. As a Christian, the way we reflect God's Glory in our vision is to make sure the images that enter through the eye gate are reflective of "The Way, The Truth, and The Life", and we are to keep our eyes focused on Him.

The vision (dreams and goals) that God gives us are to reflect His Glory. When God gives us a vision, He also offers strategic plans to accomplish the vision. He creates a path, "the process" for us to complete and achieve the dream or vision that He provides. The Bible speaks of a person who had a dream; his name was Joseph. As a child, Joseph had a dream of being in a position of authority of a ruler. Joseph was the beloved child of his father; he was more favored than his other brothers.

He told his family about this dream, and they did not believe it to be true. Joseph's brothers actually despised him more because of his dream and thought of committing homicide. Instead of killing Joseph, his brothers sold him into slavery where an Egyptian officer of Pharaoh named; Potiphar purchased him. God was with Joseph while he was a slave at Potiphar's house. Every task Joseph completed was successful because God was with him. Even though Joseph was in slavery, God was continually creating the path for Joseph's dream to come to fruition. During his time as a slave in Potiphar's house; Joseph was wrongfully accused and forgotten, but his gift brought him before Pharaoh. While you are on the path to achieving your God-given dream, you will encounter some situations that may cause you to be wrongfully accused, forgotten, and overlooked. Always keep in mind that your gift will bring you before great men, and even though the vision tarries, wait for it.

Pharaoh finds himself needing his dreams interpreted. He is told that there is a slave in his prison that has a gift in the interpretation of dreams. Joseph is called to come; he explains the dreams to Pharaoh and purposes a plan to counteract the years of famine that will take place in the land in the future. Pharaoh and all of his servants were extremely impressed with

Joseph's knowledge of administration. Pharaoh saw that God was with Joseph, and God had made all things known to Joseph, and the Spirit of God was with him. So, Pharaoh appoints Joseph 2nd in command, placing his authority over all the land of Egypt. Pharaoh dressed him as a ruler and gave him his authority. Even though Joseph's brothers tried to end him, his dream had to come to pass. Although he was placed in prison after being wrongfully accused, Joseph's dream came to pass. So, I encourage you, no matter what happens on the pathway to completing your dream or vision, remember it has to come to pass. When our vision is completed, this gives the Glory back to God. Although it was God's vision given to us, the witness of the completed vision reflects Him on the Earth.

"Then the Lord answered me and said, "Write the vision and engrave it plainly on [clay] tablets So that the one who reads it will run. 3 "For the vision is yet for the appointed [future] time It hurries toward the goal [of fulfilment]; it will not fail. Even though it delays, wait [patiently] for it, because it will certainly come; it will not delay" (Habakkuk 2:2-3; AMP).

The Ears

"So, then faith cometh by hearing, and hearing by the word of God" (Romans 10:17).

The function of the physical ear is to transmit sound to the brain. The inner ear converts the sound into an electrical signal for the brain to comprehend. The inner ear also assists with balance, equilibrium, and positioning, as well as balancing of the head and eye movements.[2] What we hear can affect our view in life. "So then, faith cometh by hearing, and hearing by the word of God" (Romans 10:17). The Word tells us that hearing the word of God increases our faith. And faith is what pleases God, not by the works of our flesh, but faith.

The word, faith, by definition, means complete trust or confidence in someone or something: such as a strong belief in God without proof. There was a woman in the Bible that heard of Jesus and His miraculous acts. The Word tells us this woman was diseased with an issue and she wanted to be healed. This woman suffered from this life draining issue for twelve years. She heard of Jesus' teachings; she heard that Jesus (the Word made flesh) was near and thought within herself, that if she could just touch His garment, she shall be made whole. It was the hearing of the capability of Jesus that made her believe the action of touching His clothes would make her completely healed of the life draining issue. She had complete trust in Jesus' capabilities to heal her. But the ironic thing is,

Jesus said to this woman, *it was your faith that made you whole*. Not the action of touching His garment, but the belief that Jesus was fully capable of healing. She would not have had the complete trust in Jesus if she did not hear of His miraculous works or heard of His teachings. The woman's hearing the Word produced the faith to act, and as a result, she received her healing from that very moment (Matt. 9:20-23).

Since the ears are the conduit for information to the brain, the Word tells us to *"tune your ears to wisdom"* (Proverbs 2:2). We must decipher and sift the information that is allowed into our ears. Just as hearing God's Word influences and changes our perspectives and outlook, so will hearing negative and ungodly words influence our perspectives and perception. Therefore, God wants us to cover our head with the helmet of salvation. *"And take the helmet of salvation, and the sword of the Spirit, which is the word of God"* (Ephesians 6:17; KJV).

The Nose

".... Sweet smelling Savour..." (Genesis 2:7; KJV)

Our nose transmits smell to the brain formed as impulses of information through the olfactory nerve to the brain. Certain smells can trigger memories such as Grandma's house as a child or that first love's cologne or perfume they wore on the first date or the first kiss. Our sense of smell affects our mood, emotions, and how we experience foods and eating. Our ability to smell enhances our experiences on earth.

In Genesis 2:7, after the creation of the Heavens and the Earth, God formed man. God created man from the dust of the ground, and He breathed life into his nostrils, and man became a living soul. What determines a live birth from a stillborn—the babies' ability to take in and expel air through the nose, mouth (crying), and lungs.

Wow. Right now, stop…Inhale…Exhale! Every breath you take is a testimony to God's awesome power to create, and through your very nose, God gave the first man, life. In Psalm 150:6, we are encouraged to "let everything that has breath praise the Lord." Every breath should be done with praise unto God, for this nose of ours is the very conduit in which we are counted amongst the living. So, every time you inhale, praise the Lord and every time you exhale, give God praise because you are a living and breathing witness of God's awesome creation and power.

Our Lives Emits a Smell unto God

According to consumer research, globally, the market for room refreshers and deodorizers exceeds ten billion dollars annually, and consumer spending will increase by as much as 8.8% yearly.[3] This statistic shows that as consumers, we want our dwelling places such as our home, automobiles, office spaces, and other environments to obtain a pleasant, inviting smell or a pleasing aroma when we are present. Just like us, God wants the environment of our lives to have a pleasing and inviting aroma for Him to dwell. Paul, the writer of Corinthians, writes that our lives are a Christ-like fragrance rising to God…2 Cor. 2:15 (NLT), and he also writes in Romans 12:1: *I beseech you therefore, brethren, by the mercies of God, that ye present your bodies a living sacrifice, holy, acceptable unto God, which is your reasonable service.*

But what does this image of an acceptable sacrifice look and smell like? In Leviticus, God had given instructions to Moses to tell the Israelites to give burnt offerings on the altar. God had given him instructions on how to kill the animals, which part could be burned completely, which parts couldn't be and which parts are to be handled only by the priest. God (El Shaddai) gave everyone from every socioeconomic status a resource to offer unto Himself. These offerings ranged from bulls, goats (male or female), birds, and grains (flour). The offering had to be the best, blemish free, perfect sacrifice the Israelites could offer. In Leviticus 8, Moses was given the instructions by God to consecrate Aaron and his sons as priests. Moses washed, covered, and anointed Aaron and his sons as the Lord had commanded him (Lev.8:4-13; NLT). Moses then takes three animals (1 bull; 2 ram) and one basket of unleavened bread as sacrifices as the Lord commanded him (Lev. 8:1-4). The types of sacrifices have their specific spiritual meaning and biblical symbolisms—the rams (the male lambs), unleavened bread (bread cooked without yeast), and the bull (male cow). Out of the sacrifices that were offered by Moses, only two produced the sweet and soothing aroma unto the Lord. It was the entirely burnt offering (Lev. 8:21; KJV) and the consecration offering (Lev. 8:28; KJV) that produced a pleasing, sweet aroma unto the Lord.

As believers, we are to present our bodies as Living sacrifices unto the Lord, which is our reasonable duty. The sacrificed life that smells good, that is pleasing and soothing unto the Lord, is the life that is priestly (someone whose lips keep the knowledge of the Holy One and walks by it), entirely offered (fully submitted to God), and consecrated (set aside for use) unto Him, as the Lord commanded. These are the type of lives that send a sweet-smelling aroma to the nostrils of God. These lives are the Christ-like aromas that ascend to the nostrils of God, and He says, "Ahhh, that smells just like my Son."

The Mouth

"Can bitter and sweet come from the same mouth?" James 3:11
"And the Lord said…Who hath made the man's mouth?" Ex. 4:11

Our mouths are one of the conduits by which we verbally express thoughts, ideas, and ingest foods for the nourishment of the body. It also allows us to enjoy the taste of foods; it is one of the five senses used to perceive the world. The Bible talks of the mouth in several passages of scripture, but James speaks of the tongue and mouth in detail.

Can you identify with this scenario? You have a conversation with an individual that you are not fond of. Then the discussion becomes intense, and the socially acceptable guard is down, then you say every ill thing that is on your mind about and to this person. But nobody knew what was on your mind until you opened your mouth and said it.

In the Book of James, the third chapter, it speaks about the mouth and the tongue.

3 When we put bits into the mouths of horses to make them obey us, we can turn the whole animal. 4 Or take ships as an example. Although they are so large and are driven by strong winds, they are steered by a very small rudder wherever the pilot wants to go. 5 Likewise, the tongue is a small part of the body, but it makes great boasts. Consider what a great forest is set on fire by a small spark. 6 The tongue also is a fire, a world of evil among the parts of the body. It corrupts the whole body, sets the whole course of one's life on fire, and is itself set on fire by hell (James 3:3-6; KJV).

Our mouths have the power to direct our course, change the direction of the lives of others and even create. If you don't believe me, look in Genesis 1:3, *God said let there be light*, and there was light and still is light until this very day. Throughout Genesis, the first chapter, we see where God said and it happened. We also see in chapter two of Genesis where God gave Adam authority to name the animals and whatever Adam names the animal, *its name shall remain* (Genesis 2:19; KJV). Since we are made in His image, we have the same power of speech as God.

The words in our mouths carry responsibility and a penalty so much so that in the Day of Judgment, we will have to give an account of the words we have said throughout our lifetime.

"I say unto you, that every idle word that men shall speak, they shall give account thereof in the Day of Judgment" (Matthew 12:36; KJV).

I know that I (we) can say some silly or hurtful things in the heat of the moment, but recognizing this scripture makes us more aware of what we say, especially when we will be held accountable. Let us use our mouths to speak of God's goodness, give God glory, and speak the truth of God's words. Let us speak life to dead things, speak well of others, speak testimonies of victory, for these things we can be acquitted of judgment in the last day.

Chapter 2 challenge:

Over the next three days, pay attention to how many negative words you hear, see, and say. Compare them to the number of times you hear, see, or say words of positive praise to God and others.

If the number of negative words supersedes the number of positive words, go to God in prayer about this issue of your heart.

Chapter 3

The Heart of the Matter

"Blessed are the Pure in Heart for they shall see God" (Matthew 5:8; KJV).

The heart is the "Pump" of the body. It pushes oxygenated blood to every organ in the body. Many factors can affect the heart's health such as hypertension, high cholesterol, smoking, prolonged stress, and weight gain. All of these factors increase the chances of a heart attack. The body cannot live without the pumping action of the heart. Even after a person is considered to be brain dead, the heart is active for a short period of time because of the heart's intrinsic beating action.[4]

"For the life of the flesh is in the blood..."- *(Leviticus 17:11; KJV)*
Just as the physical heart pushes blood throughout the body, the spiritual heart pushes life throughout the spiritual body. The heart is the center point of all spiritual activity. In Matthew chapter five, Jesus gets away from the crowd and goes up to the mountain; later, his newly-formed disciples came to Him. On the mountain, away from the crowds, Jesus began to teach the disciples how to experience the "Supreme Blessedness." It's the

isolated; intimate time alone with Jesus that yields optimum teachings. The opportune time to absorb these lessons is when you are isolated from the busyness of the crowds and your everyday occupations. These lessons, the Beatitudes or Sermon on the Mount, are taught to the disciples to help them experience supreme blessedness while here on earth. Jesus teaches about mourning over sin, meekness, hunger for righteousness, the blessing of the merciful and the peacemaker, but in Matt. 5:8: *Blessed are the pure in heart: for they shall see God.*

How does the condition of the heart affect the sight? In Jeremiah 17:9: *The heart is deceitful above all things and the heart is desperately wicked, who can know it?* Have you found yourself holding a grudge or secretly coveting another's social or socioeconomic status? Have you found yourself coveting the ministry call or the anointing of your own family members? We all can identify with some character flaws such as jealousy, comparing, self-centeredness, hatred, racism, etc.; all of these are evidence of a heart that is not pure. In the book Genesis, we see the perfect example of what a heart that is not pure can do to a family. After God kicks Adam and Eve out of the Garden of Eden, they bore two sons, Cain and Abel. Abel was a keeper of sheep but Cain was a tiller of the ground. The time came for the brothers to give an offering unto the Lord. Cain gave the fruit of the ground (Gen 4:3; KJV), Abel offered the firstborn of his flock (Gen. 4:4, AMP). The Lord accepted Abel and his offering but had no respect for Cain or his offering. Cain became upset because the Lord did not accept him or his offering. The Lord asked Cain why he is angry and upset. If he does what God requires, won't he be accepted also? (Gen. 4:7; AMP). Then God even gives Cain a warning, *"But if you refuse to do what is right, then watch out! Sin is crouching at the door, eager to control you. But you must subdue it and be its master"* (Gen 4:7; NLT). Apparently, Cain did not take heed to the caution of the Lord because he later kills his brother, Abel (Gen. 4:8). The heart is so tricky that the only being who is capable of judging it accurately is the Lord. *I, the Lord, search the heart, I test the mind, even to give every man according to his ways, according to the fruit of his doings* (Jeremiah 17:9).

How many times have you said to yourself, "I thought I was over this?" Only to realize there is some residual animosity or jealousy about a situation or person that still lingered. I call this repeated recognizing the "fluffing up" of the heart to see what is in there, but the Bible calls it the trying of the reins of the heart by the Lord. God is so good and He loves us so much, that He would not allow us to walk around thinking we are fully recovered when we are not. We would be performing rather than living in truth. The Lord allows for testing and situations to show us what is really in our hearts so that we could ask Him for help. If Cain had simply asked God to cleanse his heart and show him how to have dominion over the sin that waited at the door of his heart; God would have accepted his offering. But Cain did not ask for God' help and as a result he killed his brother (Gen. 4:2-8).

Experiencing the supreme blessedness from a pure heart doesn't come easy. Since we are born in sin, we are inheritably sinful, with sinful behaviors, wicked thoughts, and a corrupt heart; a pure and clean heart must be created by God. Even the psalmist and King David, "a man after God's own heart," asked God to "create in me a clean heart" (Psalms 51:10). The word, "create," is interpreted as to come into being as something unique that would not naturally evolve, or that is not made by an ordinary process. The definition of "create" implies the making of newness. To have a heart that is unlike the previous heart, this new heart must be made by God. We cannot change our hearts, only the power of God and the Holy Spirit can transform the heart of man. The Bible says that the king's heart is in the hand of the Lord, as the rivers of waters, he turns it whithersoever he wills (Proverbs 21:1). Our heart determines our outlooks or demeanor, the way we experience Him, and the blessings He gives to us. Just as blood cannot adequately flow through a clogged artery, likewise God cannot allow His Spirit through a heart that is clogged with envy, strife, deceit, anger, hatred, wrath, slothfulness, offenses, perversion, and disobedience.

So, how can you obtain a created clean heart? Accept the Lord as your Saviour, walk and talk with Him daily in prayer, meditation, and the reading of His word. The Lord will begin to reveal things about your heart to you that are not becoming of Christ. The longer you walk with God, the more He will show you the contents of your heart, therefore, creating that clean heart that David speaks of in Psalms 51:10. I'll share a personal testimony of how God can show you there is an issue with your heart. We were in a revival at my home church, and the speaker was preaching of Moses and his encounter with the burning bush in Exodus 3:2-5, where God told Moses to take off his sandals because the place he was standing is a holy ground. The speaker told the audience that God had Moses remove his sandals because the sandal was the thing that separated him from standing on the holy ground. Those words stayed with me; they kept coming back into my mind and rang in my spirit for days. The very next time I went to a different church, it was a different speaker, with a different scripture text; the same word—"Remove your sandals."

"Then the Commander of the Lord's army said to Joshua, "Take your sandal off your foot, for the place where you stand is holy." And Joshua did so (Joshua 5:13-15). I knew that this was no coincidence; I knew this word was a confirmation of the need for a "spiritual bypass surgery" of my heart.

During the altar call, I went up for prayer; the Lord revealed unto me that my heart was the thing that was separating me from experiencing the "Supreme Blessedness" Jesus spoke of to the disciples in "The Beatitudes". I had to repent and ask God to create in me a clean heart, a heart unlike the previous one.

So, my advice to you is to examine what is repeatedly happening to you. If there is always a personality type that you bump heads with, or you find yourself in the same situation time after time, over and over, ask God to reveal to you the status of your heart. If you always end up with bitterness and resentment after an encounter with people—check your heart. The heart allows whatever issue that lies within it to be manifested on the outside of it, in public view. The heart attracts whatever is in it—to itself; seeds of the same kind.

One morning, while I was getting dressed for work, the Lord spoke to me about two heart types, The *Pharisaical* heart and the *Cathartic* heart. The pharisaical heart is the heart that judges; it holds grudges, it keeps up the appearance of being a Christian, but is not interested in the core truth and values of God's words and His ways. The pharisaical heart only wants to be better than; it says the right things but lacks the actions, power, and ability (anointing) behind it. The Cathartic Heart could allow for impurities to flow out; it's open to hear and consider truth. The Cathartic Heart will not become clogged with the impurities of bitterness, hatred, and self – righteousness because of the constant flow of what is not needed to leave out. The Lord told me that I needed Cathartic Heart because holding on to bitterness will cause me to become stagnate and have a stinky spirit. Keeping the heart pure before God requires constant and honest communication about how situations affect you and staying in His presence so that He can heal you of whatever ailments your heart holds.

Our lives reflect God's Glory through the evidence of having a clean heart and a right spirit.

"Guard your heart above all else for it determines the course of your life" (Proverbs 4:23; NLT).

Chapter 3 Challenge: Write the names of people or situations you often find you are feeling downcast or angry about. Pray about these people or problems for seven days. During your prayer time, ask God to reveal to you the root of the problem and ask Him to remove it from your heart.

Chapter 4

The Digestive Tract

"Anything you eat passes through the stomach and then goes into the sewer." (Matt.

15: 17; NLT)

The natural use of our Stomach is to break down the food we ingest, so

the body can receive the vitamins and nutrients from the food before the

by-products of the food breakdown are expelled as waste. The Bible

speaks very little about the stomach. The scriptures that specifically

mention the word stomach or belly are:

"Food is for the stomach" (I Corinthians 6:13; KJV)*, "A little wine for the*

stomach" (I Timothy 5:23; KJV)*, "Food passes into the stomach and is eliminated"*

(Matthew 15:17; KJV) and *"Their God is their belly"* (Philippians 3:19; KJV).

Let us focus on *"Whose end is destruction, whose God is their belly, and whose glory*

is in their shame, who mind earthly things" (Philippians 3:19; KJV). In this

scripture, Paul talks about pretentious believers that are really deceivers

with selfish ambitions, whose agenda is self-gain. They are not really

followers of Christ; they are in the group but not of the body. These are

people who only seek to give to themselves and selfishly feed the appetite of their flesh. Think about it, how many people you know that fits this description (it may be you)? A person who takes and never gives, who does not reciprocate love, kindness, gift giving, or giving of consideration to anyone besides themselves. This is a one-sided relationship, and this type of relationship is ungodly. God is love; His word says He loves us with an everlasting love and has drawn us through loving-kindness (Jeremiah 31:3; KJV). It is to the believer that we draw others to Christ with loving kindness because we are Ambassadors of Christ.

The Spiritual stomach is also made to ingest bread daily. God tells the Prophet Ezekiel to eat the Word in its entirety. God tells Ezekiel to *"eat the whole scroll and then go speak to the house," "eat and fill your stomach with this scroll"* (Ezekiel 3:1-3; KJV). Ezekiel describes this scroll as "sweet as honey in my mouth." Every day, the Christian needs the nutrition of the word for a stronger and more physically fit spirit man. Many spiritual men and women are malnourished when it comes to the bread of life (John 6:35 KJV). Notice how God tells Ezekiel to speak to the house of Israel after eating and filling his stomach. It is important to God that we have something to give, a word of encouragement, kindness, resources, time, etc., but we cannot give what we lack. Ezekiel was told thrice by the Lord "to eat this scroll and fill your stomach." The number three (3) represents completeness when Ezekiel is told to eat this scroll three times. This signifies God telling Ezekiel to completely ingest this word so that he would have it in him to go out, speak out, and give out against the rebellious, hard-hearted house of Israel. The healthy spirit man is supposed to be able to give out to others out of abundance that he has. The healthy spirit man gives out love, compassion, God's word, because of the abundance that he has. We cannot give what we lack. My advice is to ingest the "Daily bread" every day.

"It's not what goes into the mouth that defiles, but what comes out" (Matt.15:11; KJV).

There are so many diet fads today that restrict or cut out certain foods for a certain number of days all in the name of weight management. Let's be clear, if you have issues with hypertension, diabetes, and joint pain, you should consult your medical doctor regarding your diagnosis. These restrictions from sugars, salts, fats, carbohydrates are created to detox the body. According to Matthew 15:11, it's what comes out of the mouth that defiles the man, not what goes into the mouth. If people sought God on how to detox the spirit just as intensely as seeking and creating ways to detox the natural body, the world would be better. Seeking God on how to detox one's spirit could, as a result, help drop an affinity for certain foods by showing you the why behind the cycles and eating patterns. Seek God about a detox plan that will cleanse your body as well as your spirit. There are times when detoxing the spiritual body requires abstaining from natural food for the physical body in order to rid the spiritual body (or both) of toxins. *"But this kind of demon does not go out except by prayer and fasting* (Matt 17:21; AMP). The way we show God's Glory on earth through our digestive system is to ingest nutrients that give life and energy to endure for both the physical and the spiritual body.

Chapter 4 Challenge:

Read Daniel chapter 10 and consider the number of days he fasted and the benefits of his fast.

Chapter 5

The Arms and Hands

"Thou hast a mighty arm: strong is thy hand, and high is thy right hand"

*(*Psalms 89:13; KJV*)*.

Our physical bodies possess the ability to ambulate, create, and move about in many ways (look at some of the yoga positions). God has given us the ability to reach and grasp, hug a loved one or hold our favorite drink.

Both, our natural and spiritual bodies have arms and hands too. Just as every part of the physical body has a purpose and functions along with another organ or system: every member in the Body of Christ has a function. According to Ephesians 4:13: "…till we all come to the unity of the faith and of the knowledge of the Son of God, to a perfect man, to the measure of the stature of the fullness of Christ." So, you may ask, what's the purpose of the arms and hands of the spirit man? Let's look at Christ's position on the cross, his arms and hands were stretched apart. I have read sermons suggesting Jesus' position on the cross reflects the horizontal and vertical relational direction between the believer and GOD as well as the believer with his fellow man.

But, I would suggest that the position of Jesus arms and hands on the cross reflects the all-inclusive nature of Jesus and how salvation is available to all that believe. *"For I am not ashamed of the gospel of Christ, for it is the power of God to salvation for everyone who believes, for the Jew first and for the Greek"* (Romans 1:16; KJV). The only requirement is to believe. You can reference the Book of Acts 10:34-35, the Apostle Peter tells the Gentiles, God shows no favoritism, but expresses that every nation who fears Him and does righteousness IS ACCEPTABLE TO HIM. Jesus' mission was for us all to have salvation and have access to the benefits of God through Christ that are made available to every nation, race, socioeconomic status, and to every age (absolutely everyone who believes).

Another perspective of Christ's outstretched arms on the cross is to reflect on the Body of Christ responsibility of outreach to the world. During August and September 2017, the United States experiences four major hurricanes with winds ranging from 85-185 mph, leaving destruction, despair, and repairs in its pathway.[5] After this time, many organizations came out to assist families by rescuing people from flood waters, passing out foods, and toiletries to people who lost everything in the hurricane. Natural disasters and crisis are opportune times for the arms and hands of the Body of Christ to spring into action by reaching others in need and showing the compassion of God. Helping others in need is a ministry of showing others the love of Christ and shows that the Lord is a supplier and provider of all needs, but He uses that body of believers as a conduit by which blessings flow through. *"Whatever your hands find to do, do it with thy might for when you die there is no need for work, nor planning, nor knowledge, nor wisdom"* (Ecclesiastes 8:9; KJV). The work of our hands should reflect honor and give glory to God and God will give a reward. An individual work ethic should not be based on payment, but God's work should be completed with the perspective of giving my best unto the Lord (Col. 3:23-24). By doing this we show characteristics of Christ and reveal if we are true disciples of Jesus Christ. In Acts 6:1-7, there is a complaint among the Grecians relating to some of their widows not receiving the same amount of supplies as the Hebrew widows. This was beginning to cause murmuring among the believers; they complained of showing favoritism and bias to the Hebrew widows. This issue was resolved by the apostles telling the people to look within themselves, among their peers, and choose seven men that have a good reputation, full

of the Holy Spirit and wisdom, in which we can delegate this duty of

making sure all receive supplies equally. The people ended up choosing

Stephen, Philip, Prochorus, Nicanor, Timon, Parmenas, and Nicolas as the

overseers and distributors of supplies. If these men had a reputation of

being slackers, ill-mannered, lacking the Holy Spirit, they would not have

been chosen by the people because of their reputation. Even though these

men were not preachers or disciples, they were still used to spread the love

of Christ through their works of helps to those in need.

Some members of the Body of Christ may not be on the platform or

in the spotlight teaching and preaching; some members can have the gift

of helps to make sure the needs of others are met (many members, one

body; I Cor. 12:1). Both the works of these two hands actively spread the

Gospel of Jesus Christ in the earth. According to James 1:27, the evidence

of a pure and undefiled religion before our God and father are these: to

look after orphans and widows in their time of distress and to keep

oneself unstained from the world (NIV). The way we reflect the glory of

God in outreach is to help the less fortunate and others in their times of

need.

Chapter 5 Challenge:

Actively get involved with charities in your area by donating time, monies, or gently-used clothing (yes, give away the clothes you cannot fit into anymore) to benefit the needs of the less fortunate.

Chapter 6

The Legs and Feet

"Ye shall walk in all the ways which the Lord your God hath commanded you, that ye may live, and that it may be well with you, and that ye may prolong your days in the land which ye shall possess" (Deuteronomy 5:33; KJV).

Ambulation is our independence in this world. The ability to move about without assistance is a blessing at any age. The word, "walk," is interpreted as the ability to move along on foot, to advance by steps, or to pursue a course of actions or way of life; to conduct oneself.

I enjoy looking at the determination of a toddler who discovers that he or she can stand and attempt to walk. It's too cute. The toddler's walk is unsteady, wobbly, and requires building of muscle strength to support their bodies. The more toddlers practice walking, the more coordinated their steps become, and the muscle in their legs strengthens. As the child gets older, they become more confident in walking, and falling happens less often. The adolescent child has become more confident and accustomed to walking. They take no thought in their ability; they just get up and go.

The Bible speaks of two men who walked so closely with God that they did not experience death. The Book of Genesis 5:22-24 tells us about Enoch. Enoch was the father of Methuselah and the great-grandson of Adam. Enoch had a son at 65 years old, and after the birth of his son, Enoch walked with God for 300 years before God took him from the earth. Enoch's walk with God had a generational effect on his biological and spiritual son. Enoch' grandson Noah, lived longer than he did and God established a lifelong covenant with the world through him. Enoch sowed a seed of relationship through walking with God. Genesis 6:8-9 says that Noah found grace in the eyes of the Lord, and he is described in this verse as perfect in his generation, a just man, and as someone who walked with the Lord. If walking with God had not been modeled, demonstrated, or taught before him in his bloodline, Noah would have had no point of reference, or a knowledge base to refer to concerning how to walk with God. If Enoch had not walked with God, we would not have the current benefits of a covenant with God and a reminder of the promises of God will continue as long as the earth remains.

Another biblical example of a person whose walk influenced others is Elijah. Elijah the Tishbite is introduced in I Kings chapter 17 as a prophet of God who prophesied against the Land of Israel in Somalia. Elijah prophesied to Ahab that there would be no rain in the land. Elijah says to Ahab "As the Lord God lives, I stand before Him and there will be no dew or rain during these years except by my command!"

The drought Elijah prophesied on the land lasted for three years. Elijah's introduction into the Book of Kings reads to me like a declaration. His intro includes his name, where he is originally from and his position and belief with the Lord. The word, "stand," means to take up or maintain a specific position or posture, to be in a particular state or to submit to. Elijah had a current, active, submitted posture with God which allowed him to stand or to be in the Lord's presence. Your position, posture, and ability to submit to God, will affect your walk with God. The amount of instruction God can give to you, and audibility of God's voice to your spiritual ears, depends on the position, posture, and the ability to submit to His will.

In I Kings 19:15-17, we see where the Lord tells Elijah to anoint three men for three different duties. Elijah does as the Lord commands. Elijah sees Elisha out working the field. When Elijah walked by Elisha, he threw his mantle over Elisha. Elisha left his work and ran to follow Elijah (I Kings 19:19-20). Do you think that Elisha would have followed Elijah if he did not see his walk? And yes, Elijah throwing his mantle on Elisha did have a part to play in his willingness to follow Elijah, but the word, "mantle," in its basic form, is defined as "a loose, sleeveless garment worn over clothes." There is no meaning ascribed to a piece of cloth unless you look at the one who places the mantle on Elisha and his position (Elijah). It was Elijah's walk with God that is used to influence Elisha. It was Elijah's upright posture and submitted relationship with God that drew Elisha to Elijah. The similarities in the two men—Enoch and Elijah, are the manner in which they were taken and their course of actions, the conduct of oneself, or their way of life or in other words, their walk. Our walk should become more steady and consistent as we become mature in Christ. It is the everyday processes, everyday forward movement, step by step, being yielded, guided by God, and honoring God daily, allows that us to influence more territory with God's agenda. This is how our relationship or walk with God is a witness unto all the Earth— that the Lord God lives, and before Him we stand.

Reconstructed Walk

Can you remember when you first received Christ? At first, I was super excited; I could hear songs of praise when no music was playing, and when I slept, I could hear myself speaking in tongues. God would give me dreams of exactly what is to come in my future. But over time, my excitement faded and the reality of walking with Christ appeared to me as tedious. Can you identify with a time when your walk wasn't as upright as it once was when you first believed? What actions did you seek out to correct this crooked walk?

There were times when we can habitually exhibit a behavior that is not becoming of a person actively walking with Christ. In these cases, we need to have spiritual therapy to get our walk with Christ reconstructed.

Back in April, I kept experiencing lower back pain which caused me to seek out a chiropractor. I was told that some of the vertebrae in my back moved which caused a nerve to be pinched. I began to research other methods to relieve pain other than pain medications. In my research, I found that physical exercise can help relieve pain. So, with much prayer, I began to work on the muscles in the legs and lower back. One of the side effects of having nerve compression is muscle fatigue and weakness. I started going to the gym and using the elliptical, walking on the treadmill and cycling to strengthen the lower back and leg muscles. As a result of these workouts, I noticed that climbing stairs and standing for longer periods became easier. Also, I noticed that the formation of my steps became better. The more I worked on my legs and lower back, the better form I would have when walking.

Through these workouts, God gave me a revelation, that if I hadn't experienced any back pain, I would not have sought out treatment for the impairment. When God shows you deformities in your walk with Him, you must seek Him to help you correct it. In the Bible, Saul was one who needed his walk reconstructed. Saul was a persecutor of the church, and he believed he was servicing God by killing the believers. Saul had a deep disdain for the church. He went to the high priest in the synagogues to request for letters of permission to incarcerate anyone who belonged to the Way. Saul was adamant in killing the church, and no one could stop him. On his way to Damascus, Saul saw a light flash around him; he fell to the ground, and Jesus asked him, "Saul, Saul, why do you persecute me?" Saul thought that he was correct in his actions toward the church; he had the approval from the high priest and the synagogue also supported him, but he was wrong. Saul could not see that his actions toward the church were incorrect until he was visually impaired.

In this encounter with Jesus, Saul was unable to see for three days, and he did not eat or drink. Saul was led by other men that were present during his encounter to a street called "Straight." I can see the irony in Saul being sent to a house on this street called "Straight." Saul, the person whose walk with God personified crookedness, was led to a house on the street called Straight. But think about it, isn't this pattern identical to any one of us who God calls into a spiritual relationship? We were on our way to do our regular occupations, and God calls us to a place that is the total opposite. I remember when God was calling me; I was actually in church texting to go meet up with a "friend" after service. Little did I know on that day, just like Saul, the voice of God was louder than anything, and my plans were going to be changed forever. While Saul was at the house on Straight Street, God was preparing a man by the name of Ananias to go and lay hands on Saul so that he may regain his sight. Ananias entered the house and laid hands on Saul, and he restored his sight and was baptized.

God knows exactly how to impair us to get our attention and help us recognize the need to be back on the street called straight, walking circumspectly before Him.

Chapter 6 Challenge: Consider This...

How would a body of members (the church) look if the members walked in the Spirit like a group of toddlers? What images come to your mind? What words come to mind about a body of believers that stumbles, wobbles, constantly falls on their butts and cry? Would that body of believers be attractive to you? Would this be a place you want to attend? Is this someone you would desire to become?

Chapter 7

The Reproductive System

And God said, Let the earth bring forth grass, the herb yielding seed, and the fruit tree yielding fruit after his kind, whose seed is in itself, upon the earth: and it was so (Gen. 1:11; KJV).

And God blessed them, and God said unto them, Be fruitful, and multiply, and replenish the earth, and subdue it... (Gen. 1:28; KJV)

Physically speaking, our bodies, whether male or female, normally contains organs to reproduce. The reproductive system is the system by which humans reproduce and bear live offspring. Providing all organs are present, normally constructed, and functioning properly, the essential features of human reproduction are: 1- egg; 2- sperm fertilizes the egg; 3- the fertilized egg is transported to the fetus or womb; 4- the developed embryo being planted in the wall of the womb; 5- the formation of the placenta for growth of the embryo; 6- after the gestation period, the birth of the child and expulsion of the placenta.[6]

Let us look at the reproductive system without defects in Genesis 1:28. God gives Adam and Eve the commands to be fruitful, multiply, fill the earth, and subdue it. In the beginning, we see that together, Adam and

Eve were blessed by God when He instructed them to produce, double it, spread it abroad, take over, and rule the creatures of the sky and land. God had given them this command before they had children, before the earth had produced a shrub of the field: and no plants had sprouted, no rain had fallen and there was no man to work the ground (Genesis 2:4-7; KJV). Wait…What? Now, in Genesis 1:28, we see God blessing and giving commands, and talking to plants as if they were present, but according to the scriptures, they were not tangible yet. God was speaking to Himself as the Godhead within the Trinity. He was speaking to the earth and His own image, calling them into existence before manifestation. God was speaking to potential men and women, plants, livestock, fish, fowls of the air, and creatures that crawl.

When we are born, we have the appearance of our parents, which comes from the sperm of our father and the egg of our mother. As we grow older, behaviors, perspectives, and gestures mimic our parents because we look like whom we came from and often, our environments cultivate us. Spiritually, we came from Adam and Eve who was formed by God's hands from the dust and from the rib of man, which are made in His image. Because we are made in His image, we have that same ability to speak to the skills, goals, dreams, task, and callings that are on the inside of us that are yet to be manifested. However, the conditions must be precise for manifestations. Look at the steps and stages an embryo must go through before becoming a live birth; it's a process of developing, transportation, maturation, and then manifestation.

You may be like me at this time in my life: single, unmarried, and without children (not participating in the act of producing children either—with the help of the Lord). So, for me, being fruitful and multiplying in the sense of having offspring would be considered fornication and the act sin. However, being a single person is no excuse for me not to be producing on some level. I still have the command to be fruitful, subdue the land, and fill the earth. Just as God said; "Let us make man," before man was on the Earth until the moment vegetation was present. God has ordained or purposed there to be specific gifts and callings in each of us that will come forth when the conditions are right. Once the embryos of those gifts, skills, and callings have been developed and it will be birthed in the fullness of time.

Let me not leave out individuals who are unable to have children. You may have suffered from some disease of the reproductive system. Let me encourage you; the devil has no victory anywhere at any time. There are thousands of children that need someone to love, adopt, and pour into them. God loves us and makes provisions to all times through all situations.

But…you still have the command and potential to reproduce. In Acts 8:26-39, the Bible gives an account of an Ethiopian Eunuch who was in a position of authority; he was in charge of the Queen's money. He came to Jerusalem to worship and was on his way back home reading the Book of Isaiah aloud, when God sent Phillip to him to help him decipher the Word in which he was reading. When Phillip approached the Eunuch and heard him reading the Book of Isaiah, Phillip asked, "Do you understand what you are reading?" The Eunuch replied, "How would I know unless someone teaches me?" So, Phillip explains the scriptures to the Eunuch, the Eunuch request to be baptized; the Eunuch accepts the Lord, believes in his heart and was baptized. Phillip then leaves the scene and the Eunuch leaves rejoicing.

In the scriptures, this Eunuch does not have a name; he is only identified by his physical inability to carry seed and reproduce. When he believes and receives the Word of God, he is supernaturally endowed with

Word seed. In a book called "Lesser Known Bible People," written by Jim Coles-Rous. The writer states that this Eunuch, after being baptized, returns to his land and began to spread abroad the Gospel of the Messiah that had come to fulfill the prophecy and that the Gift of Salvation was available to all that believed, and for 1,800 years, the Christian church flourished in Ethiopia.[7] You see, although this Eunuch had no physical capabilities to produce offspring, after he accepted Christ, he was able to go out, sow, and produce seeds after his own kind (more believers like himself). As believers, we all have the command to be fruitful and multiply on some level. This is how we reflect God in the earth and the body, by being fruitful and multiplying.

Chapter 7 Challenge:

In Mark 4:8, the Bible speaks of seed sown into good ground and that seed produced fruits, some thirty, sixty, and a hundred times more than what was put down in the ground. I challenge you to ask God to show you where to sow a monetary seed in (good soil), in order to have a hundred-fold harvest.

The Author's Final Words

Being Fitly Joined

He makes the whole body fit together perfectly. As each part does its own special work,

it helps the other parts grow, so that the whole body is healthy and growing and full of

love (Eph. 4:16, NLT).

Our lives are given to us by God the Father, our creator, whose footstool

is the Earth. We, who are made in His image, have been given the

command to be fruitful and multiply, subdue the Earth, and have rule over

all animals, and He has given us every seed-bearing plant of the Earth

(Gen 1:28-29).

The Lord has created celestial bodies in which He used as a visual

reminder of His covenant with Abraham, promising him, a man who had

no children, would be the father of many nations and that his children

will be just as the stars in the sky (Genesis 15:5; KJV). The Lord has

created earthly bodies in which we carry the precious treasure of God's

Holy Spirit so that everyone will know the power within is of God and not

of ourselves (II Cor. 4:7; KJV). And the Lord has given us a spiritual body,

a body of believers that have been assigned different functions just as our

physical body parts have different muscles and bones that perform a different task, which attributes to our daily living, as described in Ephesians 4:11-12, 16.

Our sole purpose in this life is to be mirrors reflecting God's Glory in every part of our body, in all parts of the Earth. Mirrors come in different shapes and sizes; they can be found in different places like your purse or vehicle, in the smelly places like the bathroom, or even broken or shattered, but when the light hits the mirror, it still reflects the light, in whatever state it is found.

There is no need to imitate the functions of other believers in the body. God has given the church different gifts to function as one:

4 There are [d]diversities of gifts, but the same Spirit. 5 There are differences of ministries, but the same Lord. 6 And there are diversities of activities, but it is the same God who works all in all. 7 But the manifestation of the Spirit is given to each one for the profit of all: 8 for to one is given the word of wisdom through the Spirit, to another the word of knowledge through the same Spirit, 9 to another faith by the same Spirit, to another gifts of healings by [f]the same Spirit, 10 to another the working of miracles, to another prophecy, to another discerning of spirits, to another different kinds of tongues, to another the interpretation of tongues. 11 But one and the same Spirit works all these things, distributing to each one individually as He wills (I Cor.12:4-11).

6 In his grace, God has given us different gifts for doing certain things well. So if God has given you the ability to prophesy, speak out with as much faith as God has given you. 7 If your gift is serving others, serve them well. If you are a teacher, teach well. 8 If your gift is to encourage others, be encouraging. If it is giving, give generously. If God has given you leadership ability, take the responsibility seriously. And if you have a gift for showing kindness to others, do it gladly (Roman 12:6-8; NLT).

As you can see in the scriptures above, God has given the body of believers many different gifts to spread about and reflect HIS glory across the earth. My question to you is, have you received Jesus as the Lord and Saviour of Your life? Do you believe Jesus lived, died, and is now resurrected; sitting at the right hand of the Father? If you have made Him Lord over every part of your body and life and if His Spirit dwells within; then you are now ready to reflect His light. There is no need to imitate other people in the Body of Christ. Instead seek the Lord to discover who you are, who He called you to be, and the gift(s) He has given to you.

Strengthen your spiritual body, and reflect His Light in all the earth. We are only to be imitators of Christ.

Go work in your calling and reflect His light.

"You were bought with a price [you were purchased with the precious blood of Jesus and made His own]. So then, honour and glorify God with your body" (I Corinthians 6:20; AMP).

Let's Us Pray

Heavenly Father, we acknowledge you as all-powerful, all-knowing, and everlasting. Lord, we thank you for creating us in your image, with abilities to create, name, decree, declare, and the authority for it be so in your Son's name. Now, Father, I ask that you make us better mirrors of your glory. Mold us into blemish-free, spot-free, reflectors of you in every area of the Body. Father, help us to do your will, help us to be better disciples, help us to build and expand the kingdom.

In the name of Jesus I pray.

Amen.

Appendix A
Diagram

The Spiritual Body

Head- The Mind Renewed by the Word of God (Romans 12:2)

Eyes- Focused on God and His Vision for you (Matt. 6:22)

Ears- Tune your ears to Wisdom (Proverbs 2:2)

Mouth- Speaking words that are acceptable (Psalms 19:14)

Nose- Praise the Lord with every breath. (Psalms 150:6)

Heart- Keeping the heart free from impurities (Matt.5:8)

Digestive- Ingesting the Bread of Life daily (Ezekiel 3:3)

Arms and Hands- Outreaching to the lost and hurting (Deuteronomy 5:33)

Legs and Feet- Walking upright before God (Psalms 84:11)

Reproductive system- Being fruitful and multiplying (Genesis 1:28)

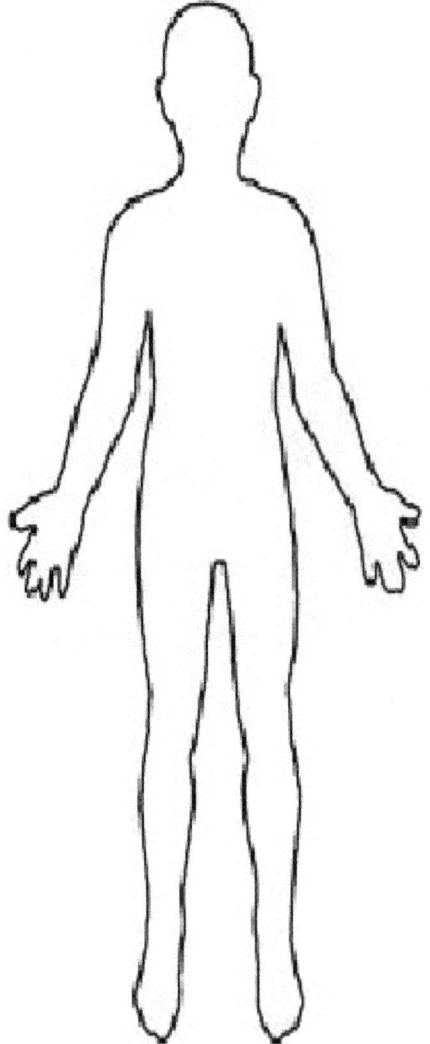

References Cited

[1] Cherry, K. "How Big is the Human Brain?"
https://www.verywellmind.com/how-big-is-the-brain-2794888/how-big-is-the-human-brain (accessed on July 12, 2018).

[2] Brownell, W.E. "How The Ear Works – Nature's Solutions For Listening." https://www.ncbi.nlm.nih.gov/pmc/articles/PMC2888317/ (assessed October 3, 2018).

[3] Market Research on Air Care Products. (2016).
https://www.euromonitor.com/aircare (accessed on July 5, 2018)

[4] Retner R., 2014, "Life after brain death"
https://www.livescience.com/42301-brain-death-body-alive.html January 3, 2014, 10:32 am ET (accessed on 10/15/2018).

[5] NOAA National Centers for Environmental Information, State of the Climate: Hurricanes and Tropical Storms for September 2017, published online October 2017. https://www.ncdc.noaa.gov/sotc/tropical-cyclones/201709 (accessed on July 5, 2018).

[6] Harrison, R. Encyclopædia Britannica. "Human reproductive system." Encyclopædia Britannica, inc.2018.
https://www.britannica.com/science/human-reproductive-system (accessed on July 25, 2018)

[7] Rous, J.C. "Lesser Known People of the Bible."
http://globalchristiancenter.com/christian-living/lesser-known-bible-people/31308-the-eunuch-of-ethiopia (accessed July 5, 2018).

About the Author

Andrea C. Dexter is a Licensed Social Worker in the State of Mississippi, a two-time Alumna of the University of Southern Mississippi in Hattiesburg MS, and a graduate of the C.H. Mason Jurisdictional Institutes' Certification Program. She worships and is a member of China Grove Church of God in Christ, where she serves as a choir member and Sunday School secretary.

"My endeavor is to encourage believers to be the person that God created them to be and not the person who imitates anyone else. We are only to be Imitators of Christ. Just as the members of our physical bodies function differently, so does our gifts and callings in Christ. Our purpose in life is to reflect God's glory in every area of the Body—in all the earth. So, I encourage you to walk in the authentic anointing God has placed on your life."

Andrea-

www.ingramcontent.com/pod-product-compliance
Lightning Source LLC
Chambersburg PA
CBHW021220020426
42331CB00003B/395